JOSH DOBBS
Chronicles

The Inspiring Journey of an NFL Quarterback, Aerospace Engineer, and Philanthropist

Norman D. Smith,

Copyright

All right reserved, no part of this publication may be reproduced, distributed or transmitted in any form or by any means, including photocopying, recording or other electronics or mechanical methods without the prior written permission from the publisher except in the case of brief quotations embodied in critical reviews and certern other noncomercial uses permitted by copy right law.

Copyright©Norman D. Smith,2023.

CONTENTS

PRESENTATION

WHO IS JOSH DOBBS

EARLY YEARS

SCHOOL PROFESSION

COLLEGE FOOTBALL CAREER

PURSUIT OF AEROSPACE ENGINEERING

SCHOOL FOOTBALL MEASUREMENTS

LEADERSHIP AND MENTORS

LEADER

SCHOOL FOOTBALL MEASUREMENTS

PRESENTATION

In the realm of expert football, there are stories that rise above the actual game. The story of Josh Dobbs is one such account. While many know him as a skilled quarterback who graced the fields of the NFL, there is something else to Josh Dobbs besides his accomplishments on the turf. This book is an excursion into the life, the energy, and the exceptional excursion of a man whose fantasies arrived at a long ways past the limits of the football field.

Josh Dobbs' story is one of strength, knowledge, and unwavering assurance. From his initial days as a school competitor at the College of Tennessee to his time in the NFL, he confronted difficulties that would have hindered the normal individual. However, it was his relentless obligation to greatness, both on and off the field, that put him aside.

As we dig into the pages of this book, we'll reveal the multi-layered parts of Dobbs' life. We'll investigate his excellent abilities as a quarterback, his surprising scholarly accomplishments as a plane architect, and his relentless obligation to rewarding his local area. We'll find the impact of family, tutors, and a well established confidence that directed him through the ups and downs of his excursion.

"Josh Dobbs: Past the Field" is a demonstration of the force of desire, schooling, and an unflinching faith in the capacity to have an effect. This book welcomes you to investigate the life and tradition of a man who tried the impossible in a literal sense, here and there the field. Go along with us as we reveal the phenomenal story of Josh Dobbs.

WHO IS JOSH DOBBS

Robert Joshua Dobbs (conceived January 26, 1995) is an American football quarterback for the Minnesota Vikings of the Public Football Association (NFL). He played school football for the Tennessee Workers, and was chosen by the Pittsburgh Steelers in the fourth round of the 2017 NFL Draft. Dobbs turned into the beginning quarterback for the Arizona Cardinals for the 2023 season following a physical issue to Kyler Murray. At the exchange cutoff time that season, he was exchanged to the Vikings following a physical issue to Kirk Cousins.

Joshua Dobbs

allude to inscription

Dobbs with the Steelers in 2018

No. 15 - Minnesota Vikings

Position:

Quarterback

Individual data

Conceived:

January 26, 1995 (age 28)

Alpharetta, Georgia, U.S.

Level:

6 ft 3 in (1.91 m)

Weight:

216 lb (98 kg)

Profession data

Secondary school:

Alpharetta

School:

Tennessee (2013-2016)

NFL Draft:

2017/Cycle: 4/Pick: 135

Vocation history

Pittsburgh Steelers (2017-2019)

Jacksonville Panthers (2019)

Pittsburgh Steelers (2020-2021)

Cleveland Tans (2022)

Detroit Lions (2022)*

Tennessee Titans (2022)

Cleveland Tans (2023)*

Arizona Cardinals (2023)

Minnesota Vikings (2023-present)

 * Offseason or potentially practice crew part as it were

List status:

Dynamic

Vocation NFL insights as of Week 8, 2023

Passing endeavors:

351

Passing fruitions:

217

Fruition rate:

61.8%

TD-INT:

10-8

Passing yards:

2,025

Passer rating:

77.6

Surging yards:

333

Surging scores:

3

Player details at NFL.com · PFR

EARLY YEARS

Dobbs was brought up in Alpharetta, Georgia, the child of Stephanie and Robert Dobbs. His mom resigned from Joined Package Administration (UPS) as a locale supervisor in corporate HR, and his dad is a senior VP for Wells Fargo. Dobbs has alopecia areata, an immune system sickness causing going bald, which initially created when he was progressing from rudimentary to middle school.

Dobbs began playing football when he was five years of age. He went to Wesleyan School and a while later Alpharetta high School.. As a senior with the Alpharetta Thieves football crew, he tossed for 3,625 yards with 29 scores. Dobbs was a three-star enroll by Rivals.com and a four-star by Scout.com. He initially dedicated to Arizona State College to play school football, however in February 2013, he changed his obligation to the College of Tennessee.

Dobbs studied aviation design during his time at the College of Tennessee. The college gave him the 2017 Torchbearer Grant, the most elevated honor for an undergrad understudy, which perceives achievements locally and scholastics. Dobbs was proclaimed as having an ideal 4.0 grade point normal and being named toward the Southeastern Gathering Scholarly Honor Roll.

SCHOOL PROFESSION

2013 season

As a genuine rookie at the College of Tennessee in 2013, Dobbs played in five games with four beginnings after starter Justin Worley was harmed in a 45-10 misfortune against the #1 Alabama Dark red Tide at Bryant-Denny Arena. Dobbs came into the game out and about at No. 1 Alabama and finished 5-of-12 passes for 75 yards. He began his most memorable profession game against the #10 Missouri Tigers at Faurot Field. He finished 26-of-42 passes for 240 yards in the 31-3 misfortune, which was the most passing yards in a rookie debut starting around 2004; Erik Ainge (118) and Brent Schaefer (123) against the UNLV Revolutionaries. After a 55-23 misfortune to the #7 Coppery Tigers and a 14-10 misfortune to the Vanderbilt Commodores, Dobbs set up a strong execution against the Kentucky Wildcats at Province Arena. In the 27-14 triumph, Dobbs tossed his initial two profession score passes and had a 40-yard hurrying score. By and large, he finished 72-of-121 passes for 695 yards with two scores and six captures and furthermore scrambled for 189 yards and a score in his actual rookie season.

2014 season

Dobbs rivaled Worley (a senior) and Nathan Peterman (a sophomore), to be Tennessee's starter for the 2014 season. Worley was declared the starter, yet Dobbs took over as the starter in November after Worley was harmed in a 34-3 misfortune to the #3 Ole Miss Revolutionaries at Vaught-Hemingway Arena. In spite of the fact that Dobbs was not driven right into it following the injury, in the next week against #4 Alabama Dark red Tide, Peterman was named the starter, yet he was feeling quite a bit better rapidly by Dobbs. Dobbs performed well in the 34-20 loss by recording 192 passing yards and two hurrying scores against the Blood red Tide. Against South Carolina, Dobbs had a breakout execution against the

Gamecocks at Williams-Brice Arena. In the 45-42 rebound win in additional time, Dobbs had 301 passing yards, two passing scores, 166 hurrying yards, and three surging scores. Against the Kentucky Wildcats at Neyland Arena, Dobbs had 297 passing yards, three passing scores, 48 surging yards, and one hurrying score in the 50-16 triumph. Dobbs and group assisted Tennessee arrive at their most memorable bowl with gaming since the 2010 season. Dobbs was named the 2015 TaxSlayer Bowl MVP in Tennessee's 45-28 triumph over Iowa. In the game, Dobbs passed for 129 yards and one score and scrambled for 76 yards and two scores. Dobbs tossed for 1,206 yards with nine scores and six interferences during his sophomore season. He completed the 2014 season with 469 yards hurrying and eight surging scores in only six games. Dobbs got two Hostile Player of the Week praises from the Southeastern Meeting, the two of which came from his joined passing and surging exhibitions for north of 400 yards in each game.

2015 season

Dobbs entered the 2015 season as Tennessee's beginning quarterback. He began and showed up in every one of the 12 normal season games and the bowl game. To open Tennessee's season on September 5, Dobbs recorded 205 passing yards, two passing scores, 89 hurrying yards, and one surging score against the Bowling Green Birds of prey in a 59-30 win at Nissan Arena in Nashville, Tennessee. In a 2OT 31-24 misfortune to the #19 Oklahoma Sooners in the Tennessee 2015 home opener, Dobbs had 125 passing yards, one passing score, 12 hurrying yards, and one surging score. In a 28-27 misfortune to SEC East opponent Florida at Ben Slope Griffin Arena, Dobbs had a season-high 136 hurrying yards and had a 58-yard getting score tossed by colleague wide recipient Jauan Jennings on a stunt play. Dobbs' score gathering against Florida was the principal gathering by a Tennessee quarterback since Peyton Monitoring got a 10-yard pass from running back Jamal Lewis in 1997 against Arkansas. Against the opponent #19

Georgia Bulldogs, Dobbs had a season-high 312 yards passing and three scores to oblige 118 hurrying yards and two scores. His endeavors in the game drove Tennessee to their most memorable success over the Bulldogs beginning around 2009. Against the #8 Alabama Red Tide in their yearly competition game, Dobbs had 171 yards passing and one passing score in the tight 19-14 misfortune at Bryant-Denny Arena. Against rival South Carolina, Dobbs passed for 255 yards and two scores in the 27-24 home triumph. Dobbs drove Tennessee to a 9-4 record, which was the most wins for the Tennessee program beginning around 2007. The 2015 season was finished with a 45-6 triumph over the #12 Northwestern Wildcats in the 2016 Outback Bowl. In the bowl game, Dobbs had two surging scores.

2016 season

Dobbs entered the 2016 season as Tennessee's beginning quarterback in his last time of university qualification. He began and showed up in each of the 12 normal season games and the bowl game. Dobbs began the season with a strong presentation in a home game against Appalachian State. In the 20-13 additional time win, Dobbs had 192 yards passing however bobbled on the objective line; the ball was recuperated by colleague and running back Jalen Hurd to give Tennessee the go on score. In the 2016 Pilot

Flying J Fight at Bristol, Dobbs three passing scores to oblige two surging scores. In a 38-28 rebound triumph over the #19 Florida Gators, Dobbs had 319 yards passing, four passing scores, 80 hurrying yards, and a surging score to lead the Workers to their most memorable success over the Gators starting around 2004. Against #25 Georgia, Dobbs had 230 yards passing, three passing scores, and a hurrying score to win 34-31. Dobbs' last score was a Leap of faith toss to wide recipient Jauan Jennings as time lapsed. The triumphant play is referred to by a lot of people as the "Dobbs-Nail Boot". With the triumph, Tennessee was 5-0 with Dobbs as quarterback and positioned as high as top 10 in certain surveys. In a 2OT 45-38 misfortune to the #8 Texas A&M Aggies at Kyle Field, Dobbs had a season-high 398 passing yards and one passing score. What's more, he got a getting score from Jauan Jennings, his subsequent profession getting score. Dobbs proceeded with strong exhibitions over the remainder of the time: he had five scores, 223 passing yards and 190 surging yards in a 63-37 win over Missouri and 340 passing yards in a 45-34 misfortune against Vanderbilt at Vanderbilt Arena. Regardless of his play, Tennessee blurred from their 5-0 beginning to end 8-4.

In the last round of his Tennessee profession, Dobbs drove the Workers past the #24 Nebraska

Cornhuskers by a score of 38-28 in the 2016 Music City Bowl at Nissan Arena in Nashville. He had 291 passing yards, one passing score, 11 scrambles for 118 yards, and three hurrying scores. Dobbs was named the MVP of the game.

Dobbs drove Tennessee to a second back to back 9-4 record. Tennessee's 18 successes with Dobbs in charge were the most for the school north of a two-year length starting around 2006-2007.

Dobbs was accepted into Omicron Delta Kappa at Tennessee in 2016.

COLLEGE FOOTBALL CAREER

Josh Dobbs' school football profession was completely remarkable, set apart by his ability as a quarterback, his initiative on and off the field, and his capacity to adjust sports and scholastics. Here is an inside and out take a gander at his school football venture:

Enlistment at the College of Tennessee:

Joshua Dobbs, ordinarily known as Josh, started his school football profession at the College of Tennessee, where he had a huge effect. He showed up nearby with a profound energy for the game and an assurance to succeed. His enlistment at Tennessee denoted the start of a wonderful excursion in school football.

Features of His School Football Career:
As a quarterback, Josh Dobbs showed striking abilities and football intelligence level. He was known for his precision, arm strength, and capacity to make urgent plays under tension. Dobbs' school vocation was interspersed by extraordinary minutes, including game-dominating scores and great passing records.

One of the most essential snapshots of his school profession was the "Leap of faith" pass he finished to Jauan Jennings to overcome the College of Georgia in

2016, a play that has become famous in Tennessee football history.

Dobbs additionally set standards for absolute offense and scores, hardening his standing as quite possibly of the most achieved quarterback throughout the entire existence of the College of Tennessee.

Influential positions and Accomplishments:
Josh Dobbs was a skilled quarterback as well as a characteristic chief. He gained the appreciation of his colleagues and mentors through his hard working attitude, commitment, and rousing initiative style. His

colleagues frequently admired him as a good example both on and off the field.

Dobbs' initiative stretched out past the sport of football. He was named a group chief and was instrumental in persuading and directing his kindred players. His capacity to resist the urge to panic under tension and rouse his group during testing minutes was a sign of his initiative.

Scholarly Achievements:
One of the most wonderful parts of Dobbs' school vocation was his commitment to scholastics. He sought after a degree in advanced plane design, a field

known for its thorough requests. Adjusting the requests of a Division I football program with the scholastic thoroughness of designing is very difficult, yet Dobbs figured out how to succeed in the two domains.

His obligation to training and his progress in such a requesting major procured him acknowledgment as a star competitor as well as a researcher competitor. This double responsibility exhibited his discipline and assurance, setting a norm for hopeful competitors seeking after advanced education.

Progress to the NFL:

Following his effective school football vocation, Dobbs entered the NFL draft, eventually understanding his fantasy about playing proficient football. His school encounters, both as a competitor and an understudy, set him up for the difficulties and chances of the NFL. His time at the College of Tennessee filled in as an establishment for the following period of his football process.

All in all, Josh Dobbs' school football vocation was a demonstration of his excellent ability, administration characteristics, and steadfast obligation to the two games and scholastics. His heritage at the College of Tennessee keeps on motivating hopeful competitors to take a stab at greatness, on the field as well as in all parts of life.

PURSUIT OF AEROSPACE ENGINEERING

Josh Dobbs' quest for aviation design close by his school football profession is a wonderful story of devotion, knowledge, and the capacity to at the same time succeed in two requesting fields. Here is an itemized investigation of his excursion in aviation design:

Picking Aviation Engineering:
Dobbs' choice to study aeronautic design displayed his enthusiasm for information and his obligation to a field known for its intricacy and high scholarly requests. Advanced plane design includes the plan,

33

improvement, and support of airplane and shuttle, and it requires serious areas of strength for an of science, physical science, and designing standards.

Adjusting Scholastics and Athletics:

The most outstanding part of Dobbs' quest for aeronautic design was his capacity to adjust the thorough requests of the major with the tedious responsibilities of school football. Understudy competitors frequently face a daunting struggle in overseeing both their scholarly obligations and their athletic vocations, however Dobbs figured out how to succeed in the two areas.

His obligation to scholastics was an impression of his discipline and time usage abilities. While large numbers of his friends might have picked less requesting majors, Dobbs stayed determined in his mission to seek after a field that profoundly intrigued him.

Scholastic Achievements:

Dobbs' scholastic accomplishments in aeronautic design were a demonstration of his scholarly ability. He finished his coursework as well as succeeded in it. His capacity to accept complex designing ideas and apply them to certifiable issues featured his scholarly insight.

His outcome in aeronautic design collected acknowledgment inside the scholarly local area as well as among trying understudy competitors who found in him a model of greatness on and off the field.

Influence on Future Aspirations:
Dobbs' quest for aviation design was an optional interest as well as a potential profession way. The information and abilities he acquired in the field could open entryways past his football profession. His designing foundation gave him a one of a kind point of view on critical thinking and development.

The mix of his football gifts and designing instruction put him aside, making him a multi-layered person who could make huge commitments to the two fields.

All in all, Josh Dobbs' quest for aeronautic design during his school years was a demonstration of his scholarly interest, discipline, and assurance. It displayed his capacity to succeed in two unmistakably testing fields and filled in as a motivation yearning for understudy competitors and researchers. Dobbs' story is an update that with enthusiasm and commitment, one can accomplish greatness in different everyday issues.

SCHOOL FOOTBALL MEASUREMENTS

Season	Games		Passing						Rushing			
	GP	Record	Cmp	Att	Pct	Yds	Y/A	TD	Int	Att	Yds	Avg	TD

Tennessee Workers

2013	5	1-4	72	121	59.5	695	5.7	
	2	6	38	189	5.0	1		
2014	6	3-3	112	177	63.3	1,206	6.8	
	9	6	104	469	4.5	8		
2015	13	9-4	205	344	59.6	2,291	6.7	
	15	5	146	671	4.6	12		
2016	13	9-4	225	357	63.0	2,946	8.3	
	27	12	150	831	5.5	13		

Career 37   22-15 614   999   61.5   7,138 7.1
        53   29   438   2,160   4.9   34

NFL JOURNEY

Josh Dobbs' NFL venture was a demonstration of his flexibility, versatility, and his quest for greatness in proficient football. Here is an exhaustive investigation of his NFL profession:

Entering the NFL:

After a fruitful school football profession at the College of Tennessee, Josh Dobbs pronounced for the NFL draft. He was chosen by the Pittsburgh Steelers in the fourth round of the 2017 NFL Draft. This obvious the start of his expert football venture.

Newbie Season and Early Experiences:

Dobbs' newbie season in the NFL was a period of transformation and learning. He confronted the difficulties of changing from school to the expert positions, acclimating to the more elevated level of rivalry and the intricacies of the NFL game. His initial encounters included restricted playing time as a reinforcement quarterback.

Development and Development:
Dobbs' obligation to progress and his hard working attitude were clear in his nonstop development as a player. He put in the additional hours to refine his abilities and gain a more profound comprehension of the game. His commitment to dominating the

playbook and leveling up his skills as a quarterback were instrumental in his turn of events.

Exchanges and Group Changes:
All through his NFL vocation, Dobbs encountered a few exchanges and group changes. He had spells with the Jacksonville Pumas and the Pittsburgh Steelers, and his process included moves between dynamic programs and practice crews. These changes featured the unusualness of life in the NFL.

Challenges and Successes:
Dobbs confronted his portion of difficulties in the NFL, including rivalry for playing time, wounds, and the

strain of performing at the most elevated level. In any case, he likewise celebrated triumphs, including paramount game exhibitions and minutes when he displayed his abilities as a quarterback.

Authority and Group Contributions:

Dobbs' authority characteristics, which he exhibited all through his football vocation, stretched out to the NFL. He was known for his positive impact in the storage space and his capacity to rouse and uphold his colleagues. His commitments to group elements and fellowship were esteemed by his mentors and companions.

Offseason Work and Preparation:

During the offseason, Dobbs kept on working tenaciously on his art, planning for the impending seasons and remaining prepared for potential open doors. His offseason preparing and devotion to his job as a quarterback were vital to his NFL venture.

Inheritance and Future Prospects:

As Josh Dobbs' NFL venture proceeds, his inheritance is one of constancy and assurance. His story fills in as a motivation to hopeful football players and outlines the difficulties and prizes of a vocation in the NFL. Whether as a beginning quarterback or as a reinforcement, his obligation to the game and his commitments to his groups stay fundamental to his story.

All in all, Josh Dobbs' NFL venture mirrors the unusual idea of expert football, the commitment expected to succeed, and the enduring effect one can have through authority and strength notwithstanding challenges. His process is a demonstration of the quest for greatness in the realm of the NFL.

PROFICIENT PROFESSION

Dobbs got a solicitation to the Senior Bowl and was named the beginning quarterback for the South. He completed the game finishing 12-of-15 pass endeavors for 102 passing yards and a block attempt, as the South crushed the North 16-15. Most of NFL draft specialists and experts extended him to be a fourth to fifth round pick. NFL expert Mike Mayock extended him to be chosen in the subsequent round and NFL.com extended him to be drafted in the third round. In the wake of going to the NFL Exploring Join, he was positioned the seventh best quarterback in the draft by ESPN, the 10th best quarterback by Sports

Showed, and NFLDraftScout.com positioned him the eighth best quarterback in the draft. He went to Tennessee's Ace Day and prearranged his own arrangement of plays; 19 different colleagues likewise partook in Tennessee's Genius Day. He held exercises for six groups: the Kansas City Bosses, Tennessee Titans, Carolina Jaguars, San Diego Chargers, Pittsburgh Steelers, and New Orleans Holy people.

Pre-draft measurables

Height WeightArm length   Hand span   40-yard dash   10-yard split 20-yard split 20-yard   shuttle

			Three-cone drill	Vertical jump	Broad jump	Wonderlic
6 ft 3+3⁄8 in (1.91 m)	216 lb (98 kg)	32+5⁄8 in (0.83 m)	9+1⁄4 in (0.23 m)	4.64 s	1.56 s	2.69 s	4.31 s	6.75 s	33 in (0.84 m)	10 ft 2 in (3.10 m)	29

All qualities from 2017 NFL Join.

The Pittsburgh Steelers chose Dobbs in the fourth round (135th by and large) of the 2017 NFL Draft. He was the seventh quarterback chose, and the Steelers additionally drafted his previous Tennessee and Senior Bowl colleague, cornerback Cameron Sutton. He supplanted Zach Mettenberger following the draft.

Pittsburgh Steelers

On May 22, 2017, the Pittsburgh Steelers marked Dobbs to a four-year, $2.95 million agreement with a marking reward of $554,295.

Dobbs was named the starter for the Steelers' pre-season opener against the New York Goliaths.

After two beginnings and four appearances during the pre-season, Dobbs spent his whole new kid on the block season behind officeholder starter Ben Roethlisberger and long haul reinforcement Landry Jones.

Dobbs made his NFL standard season debut on October 7, 2018, in a 41-17 Steelers win against the Atlanta Hawks, as on the last play of the game, he stooped down for a deficiency of 3 yards.

On November 4, 2018, in a 23-16 Steelers Week 9 triumph against the Baltimore Ravens, Dobbs finished a 22-yard pass to JuJu Smith-Schuster, subsequent to stepping in for Ben Roethlisberger, who got harmed on the past play. Yet again in Week 14, against the Oakland Pillagers, Dobbs needed to step in for Roethlisberger, who had experienced a rib injury. He completed 4-of-9 for 24 yards and one capture in the 24-21 misfortune. Generally, in the 2018 season, he showed up in five games and went 6-of-12 for 43 yards and one block attempt.

Jacksonville Panthers

On September 9, 2019, Dobbs was exchanged to the Jacksonville Panthers for a fifth-round pick in the 2020 NFL Draft. Dobbs was exchanged after Bricklayer Rudolph won the reinforcement work and

Panthers' quarterback Scratch Foles supported a wrecked clavicle during the season opener and was thusly put on harmed hold.

While in Jacksonville, Dobbs partook in an entry level position at NASA's Kennedy Space Center.

On September 5, 2020, Dobbs was deferred by the Pumas.

Dobbs in 2020

Pittsburgh Steelers (second spell)

On September 6, 2020, Dobbs was asserted off of waivers by the Pittsburgh Steelers, his previous group.

He re-endorsed with the Steelers on a one-year agreement on April 19, 2021.

On August 31, 2021, Dobbs was put on harmed save.

Cleveland Earthy colors

On April 9, 2022, Dobbs marked a one-year, $1 million arrangement with the Cleveland Earthy colors. He was postponed on November 28, 2022, after Deshaun Watson got back from suspension.

Detroit Lions

On December 5, 2022, Dobbs was endorsed to the Detroit Lions practice crew.

Tennessee Titans

On December 21, 2022, Dobbs was endorsed by the Tennessee Titans off the Lions practice crew.

On December 29, with Ryan Tannehill out for the season with a physical issue and tenderfoot Malik Willis failing to meet expectations, Dobbs was named the starter for the Titans Week 17 matchup against the Dallas Ranchers. In his most memorable NFL start, Dobbs finished 20-of-39 passes for 232 yards, his most memorable profession score pass, and a capture attempt in the 27-13 misfortune.

On January 2, lead trainer Mike Vrabel reported that Dobbs would begin the Week 18 matchup against the Jacksonville Pumas. Requiring a success to secure the division, Dobbs finished 20-of-29 passes for 179 yards to go with a score and an interference. Notwithstanding driving for the majority of the game, Dobbs was sacked from behind by Pumas wellbeing Rayshawn Jenkins and bumbled the ball, with the Panthers returning it 37 yards for the go on score with under three minutes to go. The Titans lost 20-16, at last costing them a season finisher spot.

Cleveland Tans (second spell)

On Walk 23, 2023, Dobbs endorsed with the Cleveland Tans.

Arizona Cardinals

On August 24, 2023, Dobbs was exchanged to the Arizona Cardinals alongside a seventh-round pick in the 2024 NFL Draft, in return for a fifth-round pick in the 2024 NFL Draft. Dobbs entered the 2023 NFL season as the beginning quarterback for the Cardinals, as Kyler Murray began the season on harmed save.

On September 24, 2023, Dobbs drove the Cardinals to their most memorable success of the time in a resentful about the Dallas Cowpokes 28-16. At that point, the Cattle rustlers were undefeated at 2-0.

Minnesota Vikings
On October 31, 2023, Dobbs, alongside a restrictive seventh-round pick, was exchanged to the Minnesota Vikings trade for a 6th round pick.

NFL VOCATION INSIGHTS

Year	Team	Games		Passing					
GP	GS	Rec	Cmp	Att	Pct	Yds	Y/A		
TD	Int	Rtg	Att	Yds	Avg	TD			
2017	PIT	DNP							
2018	PIT	5	0	—	6	12			
50.0	43	3.6	0	1	24.0	4	11		
2.8	0								
2019	JAX	DNP							
2020	PIT	1	0	—	4	5			
80.0	2	0.4	0	0	79.2	2	20		
10.0	0								
2021	PIT	DNP							

2022	CLE	DNP					
TEN	2	2	0-2	40	68	58.8	411
6.0	2	2	73.8	8	44	5.5	0
2023	ARI	8	8	1-7	167	266	62.8
1,569	5.9	8	5	81.2	47	258	5.5 3
Career	16	10	1-9	217	351	61.8	
2,025	5.8	10	8	77.6	61	333	5.5 3

LEADERSHIP AND MENTORS

Josh Dobbs' authority characteristics and the impact of his guides assumed a significant part in deeply shaping his life and vocation. Here is a top to bottom investigation of these viewpoints:

Authority Qualities:

Josh Dobbs was a characteristic chief both on and off the field. His administration characteristics were clear in different parts of his life:

1. **Lead by Example:** Dobbs showed others how its done, exhibiting commitment, difficult work, and a

solid hard working attitude. His obligation to consistent improvement filled in as a motivation to his partners.

2. **Positive Attitude:** He kept an uplifting perspective, even notwithstanding misfortune. His hopefulness and versatility were irresistible, assisting with lifting group feeling of confidence during testing minutes.

3. **Effective Communication:** Dobbs succeeded in viable correspondence. His capacity to convey obviously and spur his partners made him a believed figure in the storage space.

4. **Mentorship:** He effectively tutored and directed more youthful players, offering counsel and backing to assist them with exploring their own excursions. His mentorship stretched out past football to fundamental abilities and instruction.

5. **Team Captain:** His colleagues perceived his initiative characteristics and chose him as a group skipper, a job he satisfied with honor and obligation.

Powerful Mentors:

Dobbs credited a few powerful guides who assumed a huge part in his turn of events:

1. **Family:** Dobbs' folks and relatives were early powerhouses. They imparted upsides of difficult work, persistence, and a solid feeling of local area. Their help and direction were central to his personality.

2. **Coaches:** His football trainers, both at the school and expert levels, were instrumental in forming his abilities and football intelligence level. They gave mentorship, strategic information, and direction all through his football profession.

3. **Academic Advisors:** As he sought after advanced plane design, scholarly consultants and

teachers assumed a pivotal part in coaching him scholastically. They assisted him with exploring the difficult field of designing while at the same time dealing with the requests of football.

4. **Peers and Teammates:** His companions and partners likewise filled in as tutors, offering significant bits of knowledge and encounters that added to his development as both a player and an individual.

5. **Role Models:** Dobbs gazed upward to different competitors and individuals of note as good examples.

Their accounts and achievements enlivened him to take a stab at significance in his own life.

The direction and mentorship Dobbs got from these compelling figures assisted him with fostering the authority characteristics and assurance that characterized his profession. Their help and exhortation added to his prosperity on and off the field.

All in all, Josh Dobbs' administration characteristics and the impact of his coaches were instrumental in molding his personality and directing him through the difficulties of his life and profession. Their help and direction assisted him with becoming an effective competitor as well as a positive good example and motivation to other people.

PERSONAL LIFE

Josh Dobbs' own life gives knowledge into the man behind the football cap and advanced plane design course books. Here is an itemized investigation of his own life:

Family and Background:
Josh Dobbs was brought into the world in Alpharetta, Georgia, and his family assumed a huge part in his childhood. His folks and kin gave a strong and supporting climate for his own and proficient turn of events. Their upsides of difficult work, schooling, and local area were imparted in him since the beginning.

Individual Interests and Hobbies:

Past football and aviation design, Dobbs had different individual interests and leisure activities. He was known to be an energetic peruser, partaking in a great many books and writing. This scholarly interest was an impression of his energy for learning.

As well as perusing, Dobbs had an adoration for the outside. Climbing, setting up camp, and other open air exercises were among his #1 leisure activities. These pursuits permitted him to unwind and revive in the midst of the requests of his expert profession.

Confidence and Values:

Dobbs has been open about his Christian confidence, and it has been a core value in his life. His confidence assumed a critical part in his own qualities and how he moved toward his profession. He frequently refered to his confidence as a wellspring of solidarity and inspiration during testing times.

Local area Involvement:

We've previously talked about Dobbs' obligation to local area inclusion and generosity, yet it's important that his own life was intently attached to his longing to offer in return. His veritable craving to have a constructive outcome on the existences of others was well established in his personality.

Job as a Mentor:

Dobbs' own life stretched out to his job as a guide and good example for youngsters. He effectively participated in coaching programs and tried to rouse and direct the cutting edge to seek after their fantasies and arrive at their maximum capacity.

Equilibrium of Individual and Expert Life:

Keeping a harmony between his own life and the requests of being an expert football player and plane architect was without a doubt a test. Be that as it may, Dobbs showed a capacity to successfully deal with these parts of his life. His commitment to family, confidence, and local area association added profundity to his personality and inspiration to his vocation.

Relationships:

While explicit subtleties of his own connections may not be well known, his family and dear companionships were without a doubt a wellspring of solidarity and backing all through his excursion. Dobbs' own life was set apart by his associations with the individuals who shared his qualities and desires.

All in all, Josh Dobbs' own life was an impression of his multi-layered character. Past the football field and the study hall, he was an individual of profound confidence, solid qualities, and a promise to offering in return. His own life gave the establishment to his expert achievement and made him a motivation to others taking a stab at greatness in all parts of life.

LEGACY AND IMPACT

Josh Dobbs' inheritance and effect are expansive, stretching out past the football field and aviation design. His labor of love has left an enduring engraving on different features of society. Here is a far reaching investigation of his heritage and effect:

Motivation and Job Model:
One of the main parts of Josh Dobbs' heritage is his job as a motivation and a good example. His excursion from a school competitor to an aviation design specialist and NFL quarterback fills in as a wellspring of inspiration for youthful people trying to succeed in different spaces. His capacity to adjust sports and

scholastics while keeping a pledge to local area administration grandstands the conceivable outcomes of assurance and commitment.

Local area Commitment and Philanthropy:

Dobbs' charitable endeavors and obligation to local area commitment straightforwardly affect the existences of innumerable individuals. He has made instruction, STEM projects, and youth mentorship more available, giving open doors to underserved networks. His work in misfortune help and local area improvement has likewise exhibited his readiness to have a substantial effect on the planet.

Commitment to STEM Education:

As an aeronautics designer, Dobbs has added to the field of STEM schooling by effectively advancing its significance and openness. He has drawn in with understudies and associations to cultivate an interest in science, innovation, designing, and math. His support for STEM instruction has made a pathway for youthful personalities to investigate these basic fields.

Character and Leadership:

Dobbs' initiative characteristics, both on and off the field, have impacted his colleagues, mentors, and companions. His personality, hard working attitude, and faithful obligation to greatness have made a permanent imprint on those he has experienced all through his excursion.

Adjusting Numerous Passions:

Dobbs' capacity to effectively adjust the requests of being an expert competitor and an aviation design specialist has shown others that they need not restrict themselves to a solitary energy or profession. His story is a demonstration of the force of chasing after different interests and declining to be bound by ordinary assumptions.

Confidence and Values:

His Christian confidence, values, and the significance of local area have been at the center of his personality. These convictions have molded his life as well as roused others to incorporate their confidence and values into their interests.

Future Impact:

Josh Dobbs' heritage is ready to keep developing and having an effect. As he advances in his vocation and individual life, he can possibly motivate more people to go after greatness and reward their networks.

Taking everything into account, Josh Dobbs' inheritance and effect are portrayed by his assorted accomplishments, obligation to support, and the motivation he has given to the people who have followed his excursion. His story is a demonstration of the possibility that one individual can have a massive effect on the world through their enthusiasm, difficult work, and devotion to having a constructive outcome.

COMMUNITY INVOLVEMENT AND PHILANTHROPY

Josh Dobbs' obligation to local area contribution and generosity is a characterizing part of his personality. All through his vocation, he has effectively added to different magnanimous drives and had a constructive outcome on the existences of others. Here is a definite investigation of his local area contribution and humanitarian endeavors:

Local area Engagement:

Josh Dobbs has reliably drawn in with the networks where he resided and worked, leaving an enduring positive effect. He figured out the significance of offering in return and effectively looked for chances to have an effect. His people group contribution was set apart by his certifiable longing to work on the existences of those out of luck.

Generous Initiatives:

Dobbs was engaged with a scope of humanitarian drives, including yet not restricted to:

- **STEM Education:** His experience in aviation design drove him to zero in on advancing STEM (Science, Innovation, Designing, and Math) training. He worked with schools and associations to urge understudies to seek after STEM subjects, facilitating studios and occasions to ignite their advantage in these fields.

- **Youth Empowerment:** Dobbs was areas of strength for a for youth strengthening and mentorship. He frequently tutored youngsters, sharing his encounters and bits of knowledge to assist them with exploring their own excursions to progress.

- **Local area Development:** He partook in different local area advancement projects, adding to endeavors that meant to work on the everyday environments and amazing open doors for underserved networks.

- **Calamity Relief:** Dobbs was known to be effectively engaged with catastrophe aid ventures, offering his help and assets to networks impacted by cataclysmic events, like tropical storms and floods.

Influence on Individuals:

One of the most exceptional parts of Dobbs' people group inclusion and magnanimity is the singular effect he had on endless lives. He contacted the hearts of those he connected with, rousing them to seek after their fantasies and roll out a positive improvement in their networks.

Administration in Philanthropy:

Dobbs' administration in magnanimity stretched out past composing checks or showing up. He was effectively connected with, frequently adopting an involved strategy to guarantee that his drives had a significant effect. His obligation to these causes showed that he was an expert competitor as well as a sympathetic and caring person.

Rousing Others:

Dobbs' altruistic endeavors filled in as a motivation to others in the games world and then some. He showed the way that competitors and people of note can use their foundation to make significant change in the public arena. Numerous people and associations were roused by his guide to turn out to be more dynamic in their own magnanimous undertakings.

Tradition of Giving:

As Josh Dobbs' profession advanced, his tradition of offering back kept on developing. His devotion to local area contribution and generosity turned into a sign of his personality, and his effect was felt inside the networks he filled in as well as inside the more extensive social texture.

All in all, Josh Dobbs' people group contribution and magnanimity epitomize his real craving to make the world a superior spot. His activities and drives exhibited the positive impact that people in the public eye can have, and his heritage is a demonstration of the force of sympathy and the significance of rewarding those out of luck.

END:

In the pages of "Josh Dobbs: Past the Field," we've left on a striking excursion through the life and accomplishments of a genuine renaissance man. Josh Dobbs, the quarterback, the designer, the humanitarian, and the motivation, has shown us that the quest for greatness exceeds all logical limitations. As we finish up our investigation of his life, we are left with a significant feeling of esteem for the one who rose above the constraints of his calling.

Dobbs' story is a demonstration of the force of constancy and difficult work. His excursion from a little fellow with a fantasy to an expert football player and aeronautics designer is an encouraging sign for the people who try to pursue their own desires. Through misfortune and win, he never faltered in his obligation to having an effect, as far as himself might be concerned, however for other people.

While the football field might have been where he displayed his athletic ability, his commitments off the field have been similarly significant. His devotion to training, his vigorous endeavors in rewarding the local area, and his faithful obligation to rousing the cutting edge are heritages that will far outlive his time in the NFL.

In "Josh Dobbs: Past the Turf," we've seen the man behind the protective cap, the individual who never failed to focus on his underlying foundations, his qualities, and his fantasies. His process fills in as an update that with difficult work, a hunger for information, and a merciful heart, one can accomplish significance and make the world a superior spot.

As we bid goodbye to this book, let us convey with us the illustrations of Josh Dobbs' life: the significance of commitment, the quest for information, and the force of offering in return. His story is a demonstration of the levels that can be reached when one joins ability with a tenacious quest for one's interests. Josh Dobbs has made history, and his process keeps on moving every one of us to try the impossible.

Much thanks to you for going along with us on this unprecedented excursion through the duration of Josh Dobbs. May his story move you to go after your own fantasies and have an effect on the planet, similarly as he has.